Teen

Matter

Most

A Powerful, Straightforward

Guide for Teens

Your life has purpose, and you are important!

Library of Congress Control # 1-1023359821

ISBN- 13:978-0615924144

ISBN- 10:061592414X

Connect with Stephanie Lahart

http://about.me/stephanie.lahart

https://www.facebook.com/1lahartstephanie

https://twitter.com/1lahart

http://stephanielahart1.wordpress.com/

http://1lahartstephanie.blogspot.com/

You can find me on **Google+** as well.

Interests and Expertise

Speaking to the youth in Juvenile Hall, programs for struggling teens, Churches, schools with at-risk teens, at-risk youth programs and camps, Transitional homes for teens, or any other teen programs that help in shaping, molding, motivating, and empowering our youth.

To Book Stephanie Lahart, email your request to: stephanielahart1@gmail.com.

Stephanie Lahart is also the author of:

Overcoming Life's Obstacles

Enlighten~Encourage~Empower

DEDICATION

I dedicate this book to teens ALL over the world that need to know that somebody truly cares for you; somebody is rooting for you and wishes the very best for you!

I wrote this book specifically for you! Please know this: I poured my heart into this book. Every word that I wrote is genuine. It was important for me to write from a genuine place so that every teen that reads this book would feel connected to what I was saying.

For every teen that's reading this book, please read carefully. I don't want you to skip pages. I wrote this book as a guide to help promote growth within yourself. Try your best not to dismiss anything that you read in this book. You may not get it now, but in time, as you grow as a person and change your mindset, you'll understand and appreciate this book for what it is.

Everything that you read in this book may not pertain to you. I ask that you take what's of value to you and apply it to your life. And, who knows, you can share the other information you've read with another teen that could use it!

Some of the topics that I've written about may stand out more to you than others, and that's quite okay. I challenge you to read this book to the end, page-by-page, being careful not to skip around. I don't want you to miss out on anything!

I promise to keep you engaged. Trust me, with my writing style, you won't be bored. You've got my word on that!

This teen guide is short, but VERY effective. *Teens Matter Most* will provide you with more than enough tools that will help you through your teenage years and beyond.

You've picked the right book! ~Enjoy~

CONTENTS

Love Yourself for who YOU Are

I remember what being a teenager was like. I remember it all too well. You definitely have your ups and downs. I know that I had my fair share of the downs.

Some of you reading this right now may be experiencing some of the following things: Issues with self-confidence, acne problems, having no friends, trying hard to fit in, issues with body image, or bullying. There may also be some of you dealing with the pressures of drugs, sex, and alcohol.

I want to first start out by saying that YOU are special, YOU are somebody, and YOU have so much potential and greatness in you! Please realize how important you are! Don't you ever forget that!

I know that being a teenager can be difficult and challenging at times, but I'm getting ready to share some really helpful things for you to consider and think about.

Everybody is different. We are all unique in our own way. If you're one of those people who compare themselves to others, I would strongly recommend that you don't do that. Learn to love and embrace yourself for who you are. Focus on the goodness within yourself. Focus and build on your talents and special gifts that you have within you. If you're not too happy with your looks, it's okay to branch out and try different styles. Try doing something different with your hair. Try switching up your clothes for a different look. Make sure that you take good care of your hygiene. You should put effort into smelling good. You should also make sure that your hair, nails, teeth, and face are clean and well-kept.

I know some of you may be reading this and saying to yourselves "Did she really just say that?" Yes I did. I know that you're all old enough to know better, but this is just a friendly reminder. If you take good care of yourself, overall, you'll start to feel better about yourself. You have to make an effort.

Everybody wants to feel good about themselves, so I'm going to give you some tips on what you can do to work on building high self-esteem.

Recognize what you're great at and build on that. Involve yourself in positive activities that make you feel good about yourself. Learn to be positive and speak nothing but good things about yourself. Get out of the habit of beating yourself up or putting yourself down. Give yourself credit where it's due. Remember, we all make mistakes. Don't be so hard on yourself when you make a mistake. Learn from it.

Create opportunities that you can be proud of. If you like to dance, try your best to stand out and be the greatest! Do you enjoy playing some kind of instrument? If so, play with all of your heart and soul. Stand out and make people notice you! I'm sure I have some readers who have a talent for drawing, painting, and/or sculpting. Do you realize how much skill and talent this takes? You have a gift. Share it with the world! Where are my singers at? Don't just sing in the shower or at home. Keep honing your skills and use your beautiful and powerful voice to "WOW" others! I think you get my point. Let your light shine and be great at whatever you set out to do!

Set goals for yourself. Visualize what it is you want to accomplish and go for it! Here's an important tip I want to share with you: BELIEVE in yourself and your capabilities. Don't ever doubt who you are! Get excited about your future!

Take some time to really look at YOU. I mean it. Instead of finding things that you don't like about yourself, focus on what you do like. Remember what I said earlier: Do NOT compare yourself to others. You are who you are. Keep your head up! It's important to value who you are, respect who you are, and, most importantly, love who you are! You have purpose on this earth.

I challenge you to be consistent and stick with what works for you. In time, you'll be walking around feeling great about yourself! One step at a time, you'll get there. Trust me, you will!

Teenage years aren't easy, but with effort, change, and determination, you'll become stronger, wiser, and an overall better you. Stand tall and have courage.

Choices

Choices, Choices, Choices. Let's face it, we all have to make them. If you think about it, everything that we do starts with a choice. Let me give you some quick examples of what I'm talking about.

We make everyday choices about what we're going to eat, what we're going to wear, deciding what time we're going to work-out, what time we're going to wake up or go to sleep, etc.

Now that I have your attention, I would like to discuss important things that you may have to make decisions about. As teens, you are faced with so many things on a daily basis and it can sometimes be overwhelming, exciting, and scary too.

I want to discuss your friends. Be mindful of the people that you call your friends. If people are truly your friends, they will want to see you do well in life, and they won't try to put you in a position where you can get into trouble, hurt yourself or others, or completely ruin your life by making a bad decision that will cost you big time!

Choose your friends wisely. Try to pick out people that share your same interests. It would also be wise to hang out with people who have good morals and values. I know that some teens don't give it any thought, but you should. Be careful of the company that you keep.

I'll leave you with this to think about regarding friends: Make sure that they TRULY like you and have your best interest at heart. A true friend will be honest with you and bold enough to tell you when you're wrong. They don't want to see you go down the wrong path.

These are some things that you should also consider when you're deciding on friendship: Are they trustworthy, honest, dependable, supportive, selfless, a good listener, respectful of themselves and others? There are so many things to consider. Also, here's a quick reminder: Genuine friends won't be jealous of you. Please keep that in mind. I know you'll make the right choice.

Okay, let's talk about drugs and alcohol. I'll try not to get too long-winded on you, but this is an important topic.

We all know that if you're under the age of 21, you shouldn't be drinking or using drugs. But the fact of the matter is, teens are drinking and using drugs. I will share this with you: Underage drinking and drug-use is irresponsible and you risk the chance of putting yourself in some compromising positions.

Underage drinking and drug-use can cause the following: Death, addictions, mood changes, getting arrested, getting lower grades in school, poor performance in your extracurricular activities, etc. I want you to think smartly! You can't afford not to.

Don't be pressured or fooled into thinking that everybody's doing it or that it's the thing to do. That's not true. It's a personal choice and you don't have to be a part of it. Choices, Choices, Choices! It's a part of life and I want YOU to make the best ones. You have more important things to worry about, let's not add more trouble to your plate. Your plate is already full.

Do you, or somebody that you know, like to: Shoplift, steal vehicles, burglarize homes, fight, and/or keep up trouble? Let me give you something to REALLY think about.

This kind of behavior will destroy you and your life! Some of you may be saying, "Not me, I've never been caught!" Or some of you may be saying, "It's cool or fun!" You may think it's all fun and games now, but what IF...

Could you see yourself in juvenile hall? Or, if you've already been there, done that, do you remember what it was like? I don't know about you, but I wouldn't want to be locked up being told what to do. They have complete control over you and there's nothing you can do about it. You have to follow their rules. Period, end of story.

If you continue on the road that you're going down, you'll find yourself in jail and/or prison. I want you to imagine being there for a second. I mean REALLY imagine. I don't know about you, but I'd be scared to death being in those cells with people from all walks of life. If you don't know, SO many awful things go on behind those walls. I mean awful things! Some people get raped, beat up, and/or killed. You don't have any privacy either.

I don't think you would enjoy taking showers out in the open with total strangers. I don't think you would enjoy sitting on toilets that everybody else is sitting on. I don't think you would like the food that they provide you. I don't think you would enjoy the fact that you have to share a cell with somebody that you don't even know. I don't think you would like other inmates taking or stealing your personal belongings.

I don't want this to happen to you. You don't want to make a choice that will literally ruin your life. Think about your actions and how it can cost you. Could you imagine standing in front of a Judge and he sentences you to LIFE without parole? Imagine hearing the words: I sentence you to: 10 to LIFE, 15 to LIFE, 25 to LIFE, LIFE without the possibility of parole, or DEATH.

I'm pretty sure shoplifting, stealing vehicles, burglarizing homes, fighting, and starting trouble doesn't seem so fun now. Your life is worth more than that. Think about that the next time you even think to do something that you know isn't right. It's your life! Make it count for something great! Make something of yourself!

Some teens love school, while other teens hate it and wish that they didn't have to go. Hopefully, after reading this, you will adopt a different attitude about education and see the rewarding opportunities and benefits that come from having a great education.

Let me ask you a few questions: What kind of lifestyle do you wish to live? What is your dream car? What kind of house do you want? Do you want to be able to take vacations every year? Do you want to be in a position where you can buy what you want when you want to? Do you plan on having a large family down the line? Do you want to travel the world? Do you want to be able to dine out at fancy restaurants at any given time?

There's literally a long list of things that I could've named off, but I think you get where I'm going with this. In order to do the things I've listed above and to do the things that you've dreamed about, education plays a huge role. Why, you may ask? Let me explain.

Having a great education means that you're more likely to have an excellent career that pays awesome money and you'll be able to secure a career with excellent benefits as well. For those of you who may not know what I mean when I say "benefits," here's a list of benefits that a company can offer you: Health Insurance, Dental Insurance, Life Insurance, a Pension plan, short-term and/or long-term disability, paid time off, paid sick leave, and some companies offer bonuses for their employees.

Trust me when I say this: It's no fun when you have to struggle just to get by. It's very difficult to survive on a minimum wage job. You don't want to spend your life working at a job you don't like. It sucks! You'll be unhappy, stressed, and bored. You don't want just any old job...Strive for a career! Work hard and choose something that you have passion for. If you choose your career wisely, it won't even feel like work because you LOVE what you're doing.

Take your education seriously! Learn all that you can while you're in high school. Ask questions. If you need extra help, ask for it. You have to speak up. Prepare and study hard for your ACT, SAT, and any other test that you may have to take. Challenge yourself and set goals for yourself. Pick out the colleges that you're interested in, see what their requirements are, and work toward making your dreams a reality. You've got this! You can do it!

I know many teens enjoy watching music videos, admiring and wishing that they could live like the people in these videos and have the things that they do. Well, I'm here to tell you, you can! Study hard now and play later. Get your education and keep your dreams alive. It's there waiting for you, but you've got to work hard to obtain it.

Learn, Prepare, and Soar!!! Believe you can do it and don't doubt yourself in the process. Keep your eyes on the prize! Don't allow anything or anybody to distract you. You've got goals to reach. Stay focused and driven. Remember: Study hard NOW, play later. Study hard NOW, play later! Make it happen!

Bullying

As all of you are aware, bullying has gotten way out of control and it is ruining teens' lives and they are taking their own lives. It has to stop and we ALL have to do our part to help!

If you are one of those teens that likes to bully, please listen to me carefully. Bullying is NOT cool! No matter what you may think. You need to take a good look at yourself and search within yourself to see and understand why you do the things that you do to hurt others. Could it be that you've been hurt, bullied, or abused by somebody else? Teens who bully tend to have issues themselves such as: social problems, emotional problems, and they may be experiencing and/or have experienced mental and physical abuse. Some teens who bully have anger issues as well. There are actually a lot of things that can cause one to bully others.

It's important to be honest with yourself. Have you taken the time to think about why you bully others? I encourage you to do that. Ask yourself the question. There's a cause and effect to everything. Something is causing you to be mean and insensitive toward others. You need to search yourself, find the root-cause, and get help for yourself. Hurting others is simply NOT okay!

If you are or have been bullied, don't be afraid to speak out, get help, and stand up for yourself. You don't deserve being treated like that. You shouldn't be afraid to go to school, hang out with your friends, walk home alone, or do any other thing for that matter. You have a right to be in peace, to be yourself, and to feel safe.

As a teen, you should be enjoying your life and you shouldn't feel depressed, anxious, lonely, restless, sad, unworthy, or unloved because somebody chooses to bully you. Please talk to somebody and let somebody know what's going on. There are people who care and they will listen and help make the situation better. Please believe me! Some people REALLY do care.

Don't go through this alone. You don't have to. Please don't feel silly for reaching out for help. That's pure nonsense. You shouldn't be going through this in the first place. It's not right! Build up courage and talk about it. We have too many teens taking their own lives because they just couldn't take it anymore. I don't want that to happen to you. I want you to live your life and feel FREE! Make a vow to yourself today that you will not be bullied anymore. You will get the help that you need. Do it for yourself! Your life is worth it!

For those of you who witness bullying, please do your part to help bring an end to bullying once and for all. Here are some ways that you can help out: Let an adult or somebody who's in charge know what's going on, encourage the person that is doing the bullying to stop, talk to the person who is being bullied and encourage them to get help from somebody who can make this stop. A teacher, counselor, or any adult should be able to help. My point is this: Don't just sit back and watch this happen. Your voice is powerful. Use it.

Together we can bring about a change. There's one last thing I want you to consider: What if it was you being bullied? I'm sure you'd want somebody to take up for you if you didn't have the strength or courage to do so. Think about it! Do your part. Don't allow one more person to be bullied and you not do anything about it. Do what's right.

Your Environment

Are you one of those teens who come from a broken family? Are you being raised by one parent? Are you being raised by another family member? Are you or have you been in foster-care? Do you have both parents, but your household is dysfunctional?

I want to first start out by saying that you can be anything that you want to be. Don't you ever limit or second guess yourself. You may not come from the best environment, but that doesn't mean that you can't be something great! It may be a bit of a challenge, but I encourage you to set high standards for yourself in spite of what things look like.

If you don't like how you're living and it just doesn't seem fair, let that be your motivation and drive to do better for yourself. Pay attention to your surroundings. What do you see? What do you hear? Is this what you want for your future? If not, then strive for greatness in your life. Don't allow your circumstances to consume you. Let them inspire you to go far in life and be the very best that you can be.

It's also equally important to represent yourself. Have respect for yourself. Think highly of yourself. It's important to value who you are. You don't have to do what everybody else is doing. You don't have to behave like everybody else is behaving. Strive to be a leader! You don't want to be known or labeled as a follower. You have your own mind. Think for yourself. Make sure that you represent yourself well. Represent yourself in how you carry yourself, how you speak, how you walk, how you dress, and how you respect yourself and other people. What does your personality say about you? Work on yourself from the inside out and dare to be different.

I'm going to leave you with this: If you have a negative mindset, it's time to let it go. You can't move forward and be great if you're a negative thinker. Learn to be optimistic. Expect a positive outcome about things. There's so much power in words. Even when things don't look too good, hope for the best! See yourself making it through. See yourself where you want to be and don't give up! Be mindful, determined, and persevere.

Money is valuable and needed. Money is needed to pay bills, to buy groceries, to buy gas, to pay for extracurricular activities that you may enjoy.

For the most part, teens don't think about how much money they spend or save. Here are some tips that I would like to share with you. I want you to have a better understanding about money and how to be responsible with money. Pay close attention. This will help you in the long run.

When it comes to paying bills, keep this in mind: ALWAYS pay your bills on time. If you don't, you'll have to pay late fees that will add up very quickly. Not to mention it's a waste of your money. If you familiarize yourself with your due date, you can make your payment a day or two before the due date and you'll be good to go. Also, it's important to know how much money you have in your bank account at all times. You don't want to write checks that come back as an NSF. That stands for non sufficient funds. Not only is it an embarrassment, but the bank will charge you a fee as well.

You will have many options to choose from as to how you pay your bills each month. You can opt to pay online, mail it in, or pay by phone. Choose which method will work best for you.

You don't want to spend everything that you have. Saving money is important. You never know what may take place in your life, so you want to have extra money put away for a "rainy day." This is life. Things happen that we don't always foresee.

It's important to budget your money as well. Calculate how much your bills are each month. I personally keep my bills on an Excel spreadsheet. If you have money left over, put some in your savings account, and then give yourself an allowance to buy yourself a little something. But remember, first things first. Make sure that you're always on point and take care of your responsibilities first. That's a must!

Don't spend money that you don't have to spend. Example: Don't go out and buy a new laptop when you know that your rent or mortgage is due. Some things just have to wait. When you're out on your own and you're responsible for yourself, you have to make sure that you make responsible decisions, or it will cost you.

When and if you get a credit card, be mindful of the interest that you're being charged. When you're young, it's easy to go crazy when you get a credit card. All you have to do is go to your favorite stores, swipe the card, and leave with your goodies. Not so fast! Credit is just that, credit. It's borrowed money. If you're not careful, you can find yourself in debt up to your ears.

Although it's exciting when you get your first card, be careful with your spending habits. Make sure that you spend wisely. Remember, you have to pay this money back with INTEREST. Keep that in mind. Don't go overboard. Always keep your card in a safe place. When you get your monthly statements, make sure that you take the time to confirm the charges that you made. Identity fraud is very real!

Communication and Listening

Let's discuss the benefits of communication and listening. Some teens don't know how to effectively communicate and they only listen to what they want to hear. Hopefully I can get you to understand just how important both of them are.

Being able to communicate is vital to everyday life. There are several ways to communicate: email, speeches, text messages, talking over the phone, etc. Great communicators know how to use words together and put them into sentences that flow. They choose their words wisely so that their messages are clearly understood without being misinterpreted. Most people who communicate well are also able to hold direct eye contact when needed and know how to keep the crowd engaged. Know how to communicate can also give you a boost in confidence when speaking in front of a crowd.

If you have a hard time communicating, try talking to yourself out loud in a mirror. Read from a book or whatever you choose to use. When you begin to read out loud, learn what works and sounds good to you. Project your voice so that it's clear and easy to understand. Next, practice using different tones with your voice. Go with what feels good to you. It's important to know how to use your voice to work for you, not against you.

In regards to everyday communication amongst family, use the same concepts. Communicate your feelings and thoughts clearly to one another. If you don't communicate, people won't know how you feel or what you're thinking. Don't be afraid to talk about whatever it is you're feeling. Holding your feelings and thoughts inside can affect you in more ways than one. Talk about it.

Listening is extremely important as well. An attentive listener hears everything, not some things. It's important to listen so that you won't get things wrong or mixed up. How can you follow instructions that have been given to you if you don't listen carefully? Did you know that people like listeners? People will trust you more and open up to you if they feel like you're genuine and you're truly listening to what they're saying. On top of everything else I've mentioned, you are sure to gain a lot of wisdom and insight if you listen. You'll learn a lot from listening to others. Try it!

Food-for-Thought about Sex

As an author, I felt it was very important for me to write about sex in my book. If you're sexually active, don't worry, I'm not here to judge you or to make you feel bad or embarrassed. My only objective here is to educate you and bring awareness. If you're going to have sex, I want you to be fully aware of everything.

I'm 40 years old now, but I remember the pressure of having sex when I was a teen myself. It was especially hard for me because basically all of my friends were doing it. As a matter of fact, they would brag about what they did and how they did it. It was no secret, and they didn't care who knew about it. It was like a badge of honor if you slept with a lot of guys.

I also had a lot of close male friends, and they aren't exempt either. They respected me, but the stories they used to tell me would leave me speechless to say the least. My male friends were what I call "A mess and a half!" Their goal was to get the prettiest girl and, well, you know the rest. They would tell me how they would sweet-talk girls and had them believing that they were "the only one." They would tell girls exactly what they wanted to hear.

I'm not saying that all teenage girls and boys are like this, but trust me, you do have your fair share of those who do things like this, and then some. You don't want to get caught up in something that you'll later regret. Sex has emotional ties to it. If you ask me, I would strongly recommend that teens not have sex. I know this is far-fetched, but understand this: When you choose to have sex with somebody, it takes on a whole different meaning. If you have strong feelings for the person you're with, you will most likely become emotionally attached.

Here's the problem: When and if the other person wants to break it off, or tells you that they aren't as serious as you are, there goes your feelings down the drain. You feel betrayed, used, mislead, and then all other feelings will start to bubble to the top.

Your grades in school may start to slip. Your attitude sucks because you're hurting and you can't handle it. Now you have to worry about if he or she will tell all of your business. Then you'll start to ask yourself if you were really the only one or if there were others. Now you're freaking out because you didn't use protection and you're worried about STD's. As a teen, you don't need to be dealing with all of that extra stuff. Sex can wait!

You don't have to be in a rush to have sex. Most importantly, if you have somebody that's pressuring you to have sex, they clearly don't have your best interest at heart and they're being selfish. Nobody should pressure you into having sex. That is YOUR choice!

Here are some things that I want you to consider before having sex: Ask yourself why you want to have sex. That's a valid question. Be honest with yourself. What will you gain or lose from doing this? Will this affect your life? Is the person you're considering to have sex with free from STD's and, if so, how do you REALLY know? Is this person really serious and committed to you or does he/she have other sexual partners? Don't be in denial, be aware! Are you prepared to be a teenage mom or dad? Hey, let's be real here. Accidents happen! Even if a condom is used, it can still happen. It's rare, but even if you're taking birth-control pills, there's still a very small possibility. BUT...it can happen.

Go a little deeper and ask yourself more questions: Is this person deserving of your love? Do you fully trust this person? Do they fully respect you as a person? Are they responsible? What is the character of the person that you're considering to lay down with? How many sex partners have they had before you? This is extremely important to know. You don't want to be having sex with somebody that is irresponsible and nasty! Reminder: Some people will have sex with anybody. Please keep that in mind.

STD's are very real! If you're going to have sex, I would strongly recommend that you talk to a responsible person and get all the facts. You may be saying to yourself

"I'm a teen, I can't tell an adult that I'm having sex." I'm going to share this with you: If you feel like you're adult enough to have sex, be adult enough to talk about it. Yes! I went there with you. It's better to be protected and safe. Keep in mind that there are some things you can't get rid of. I had a close friend pass away from AIDS. We were all shocked. He only fooled around with gorgeous women. How could this happen to him? That is a point I want to make. You can't just go off of how somebody looks. You don't know what a person has just by looking at them. You never know!

YOU have a responsibility to protect yourself. I'm going to say it again: If you're going to have sex, don't take this as a joke. It's important to educate yourself and be safe at all times. You can't afford any slip-ups. That one slip-up can cost you.

Teenage pregnancy is VERY real and the STD rates amongst teenagers aren't a joke either. When you know better, you should take the steps to do better. It's your life. It's your body. It's a personal choice YOU'RE responsible for. Don't make foolish mistakes. It won't be worth it!

For the teenage girls: Value and respect your body. You don't want to be labeled as easy, a hoe, a slut, or nasty. Remember to respect who you are and make a person earn what you have to offer. Don't give away your goodies so easily. If you choose to wait, and he can't, then that shows you just what he had on his mind. You aren't important enough to wait to him. Sex is important to him, not you. That may be a tough pill to swallow, but it's better to know upfront before it's too late. Think before you act! REALLY give it some thought.

For the teenage boys: You don't have to put on a front. If you don't want to have sex, then don't! I know some teenage boys like to brag about how many girls they've slept with and they LOVE to boast about what a girl did to them. The fact of the matter is that not all teenage boys want to have sex, and that's okay. But, if you do, take the steps to protect yourself. Do your part and make sure the girl does her part too. Don't be so quick to get to it. I know your hormones are all over the place and you just want to go there, but remember what I said, "Protect yourself!" It's a must! Make sure that you strap up ALL of the time. Not sometimes, ALL of the time. I'm going to tell you the same thing I told the girls: Value what YOU have to offer! Think highly of what you've got and don't give it away to just ANY girl.

I'm going to end on this note: If you're going to have sex, think smart and be smart. Again, I strongly recommend that you talk to a grown up. Just give it some thought. They may take it better than you think. They may be thankful that you opened up to them. I know that,

25

just like me, their main goal would be to make sure that you're protected and safe. We as adults have lived longer and we have way more experience. So with that being said, we may fuss and not be too happy with your decision, but we're sure to come to our senses sooner or later and make sure that you're okay, educated, protected, and we want to let you know that we're here for you. We only want the best for you!

Respect Your Elders

I'm pretty sure that you've heard the term "respect your elders." But, what does that really mean and why should you do it?

I know that you're a teenager now, but one day you will be an adult. As an adult you would expect kids, teens, and other adults to show respect to you. Let me give you some clear examples of what I'm talking about.

Let's fast forward. You're a grown-up now. You went to college and you majored in education. You've always known that you wanted to be a 10th grade Science teacher and now the day is finally here. There's one problem though, well actually 3. You have 3 students in your class that are always causing problems and they don't listen to you and they're disruptive in your class. You have one student that likes to talk to other students while you're trying to teach class. You have another student who's always on their cell phone texting and clowning around. And the other student has absolutely no respect for you. This student always comes to class late, never does their homework, and likes to start fights with other students.

Whenever you try to speak with the students about their unacceptable behavior, it goes in one ear and out the other. You've done all that you can do and you just don't understand why. You're a great teacher and you love what you do. You're positive, upbeat, and you respect all of your students. If only those 3 students would get it together. Your class would be awesome!

You're a grown up now, so that means you have your own family. You have 2 girls and a boy. They were so precious when they were first born, and you especially enjoyed when they were around the ages of 2 and 3. But now that they're teens, they won't listen to you, they give you attitude, they get into trouble...doing things that you've asked them not to do, they don't show appreciation for anything that you do for them, etc.

You don't know where you went wrong. You've given them everything and yet they still don't fully respect you as their parent. You're supportive and you listen to what your teens have to say. You're loving, giving, and you're active in your teens' lives. Not only that, but you go out of your way to make sure that they have fun activities to do. You take them on family vacations and everything. You're a great parent!

Okay, I've given you 2 solid examples above. Now I'm going to get into why you should respect your elders. The 2 examples I gave above are very eye-opening. I wanted to give you something to chew on. Put yourself in their shoes. How would you feel if it was you?

It's important to respect your elders because it's the right thing to do, period. You don't want to be known as the "unruly teen." That's not a good look. Respecting your elders is actually beneficial to you. You can gain so much knowledge from them. Many adults light-up when young adults asks them for guidance. Instead of causing problems, reach out to them and gain more insight on life. Remember: Knowledge is power. Your elders can teach you so much if you allow them to.

It's also important to respect your elders because you should treat people the way that you want to be treated. If you want respect, you have to learn how to respect others as well. How dare you ask for respect yet you go around disrespecting people like it's the thing to do. Not cool!

Showing respect for elders shows that you have dignity, morals, and values. Having a good character in life can take you a long way. To show respect for others is to show respect for yourself.

I'll leave you with this: You may not agree with what adults may say or do sometimes, but like I stated earlier, you will be an adult one day and you will want respect. I'm pretty sure that you won't like it if your kids disrespected you. Remember to use your manners. It shows that you have respect for yourself.

Having spirituality or religion in your life can offer you hope, encouragement, inspiration, and faith in something greater than yourself. Some people refer to it as a "higher power." I personally believe in God, but everybody has a right to believe in what they want to believe in. It's a personal choice and that's your right.

Teen years can be very stressful and challenging. Hopefully these tips that I'm getting ready to share with you will help you out when you're not having a good day or when you need to just unwind from it all.

You can try some of the following things to help you relax: stretching to calming music, meditating, exercising to some of your favorite music, or choose something that YOU have a passion for.

You can also say a prayer. For some people, praying gives them peace in the midst of whatever they may be going through. What about taking a long walk on a quiet trail? A nice bike ride is always nice. You can basically think of things that you enjoy doing that will put you in a good space. I don't care what kind of day that I'm having, give me my IPod and I'm good to go. I LOVE, LOVE, LOVE music! When I'm listening to music, nothing else matters.

I'll leave you with this: When you find yourself feeling overwhelmed, it's okay to take a step back, calm down, breathe, and take a break. Sometimes we can overwork ourselves and what we really need is to just chill for a little bit. Don't feel bad or beat yourself up if you need to take a break. We all need a break sometimes.

Be good to yourself and take good care of yourself! We only have one body, so it's important to do good by it.

Teenage Partying

Teenage partying! Boy, were those the days! I remember the excitement and anticipation of seeing all of my friends, and meeting new ones too. It was a time in my life that I lived for. I mean, what's not to like? There were plenty of hot guys, great music, laughter, joking around with each other, and it was an opportunity to be loud and crazy.

Partying can be a lot of fun! I remember I would dance all night long. I'm a dancer at heart. At the age of 40, I still try to do my thing. Dance was, and still is one of my great passions that I have in life.

There's nothing wrong with partying if you party responsibly. The problem is that many teens have taken the TRUE fun out of partying. Nowadays, some teens feel like they have to drink alcohol, use drugs, and have sex. What happened to the good ole' days when we used to party and just have fun? There was no ignorance at all. Of course we would stand against the wall praying that one of the guys that we liked would ask us to dance, especially a slow dance. Our hormones were racing like crazy. But, there were no drugs, crazy sex, alcohol, or anything like that.

Teen parties should be fun. You don't need all of that extra stuff to have a good time. Keep this in mind:

When you include all of that extra stuff, you're opening the door for something to go down.

I'm not going to sugar-coat this topic for you. There are plenty of things that could go wrong and I just want to point them out to you in case you're not aware.

When you drink alcohol, you're not FULLY aware of what's going on around you. Drinking alcohol slows down your reaction time and it affects the way you think. Believe it or not, drinking alcohol affects your brain chemistry. You become more relaxed, sluggish, and it impairs your judgment.

I want you to think about something for a minute. Do you think you're being responsible if you choose to drink knowing that your judgment will be impaired? Look at it this way: anything could happen to you when you're in a vulnerable position like this.

Somebody could slip something in your drink. You could become a victim of something horrible and unpleasant. You can become very sick and/or have a major hang-over the next day. Or, if you drink too much, you could die. I'm just trying to get you to see that what you think is fun could actually end up turning out to be your worst nightmare.

Let me share something else with you. You could be smoking and using drugs and you don't know what else was added to it. People lace drugs with something extra all of the time. So what you think you're smoking, you're really aren't. One day you may be using drugs and experience things that you've never felt before, and it can take your life because it was too strong for your body to handle. All I'm saying is this: Look at drugs for what they are. Drugs kill and destroy lives. You may think it's all fun and games, but it's not. Many teens overdose on drugs and die. It's not a joke!

I would like to talk about one more thing in regards to partying. If your parent(s) and/or guardian(s) won't let you attend a party, it's not the end of the world. It's not that they're trying to be mean and don't want you to have a good time, but sometimes it's just not meant for you to go. Some adults just have a gut-feeling that they shouldn't let you go. They see and understand things that you don't.

Let me share a quick story with you. I was 16 years old and I really wanted to go to my friend's party, but my mom wouldn't let me go. I was heated!!! I was so mad at her. I stormed to my room and I called her every name in the book. Of course it was underneath my breath. I'm not that crazy. My mom didn't play that. At any rate, I was stuck in the house on a Saturday night doing nothing.

Long story short, on Monday when I got to school, everybody was talking about what happened at the party. All I could think was, "I'm glad my mom didn't let me go." There was a lot of drinking and my friend's dad got really drunk and some things took place that shouldn't have. It was horrible! I felt so bad for my friend. She was so embarrassed. People were talking about her dad all around the school. An investigation took place and I remember the officers coming to the school asking questions.

I hadn't told my mom what had happened just yet, but I did end up asking her why she didn't let me go to the party. She looked at me and said, "I don't know. I just got a funny feeling in my stomach about your friend's dad." My mouth hung open, and that's when I shared with her what had happened at the party. She just looked at me and said, "Mothers know best! I knew it was something I couldn't put my finger on."

"That could have been me" I thought to myself. For that moment, I was thankful for my mother. She kept me from harm that night. Her motherly instincts saved me from something that I wouldn't wish on anybody.

So, the next time you get a "No" to go to a party, remember that you'll have many more opportunities to party. Every party isn't for YOU.

Distracted Driver

Some of you may be reading this and you're not old enough to drive yet, but I want you to still pay attention to what I'm about to say. This could save your life or somebody else's life.

Are you a distracted driver? Do you know what a distracted driver is? You may think you know, or you may not be sure, so I'll give you some examples of what NOT to do while you're behind the wheel. You should take driving seriously and drive responsibly at all times.

Here's what NOT to do while you're driving: Please, Please, Please DO NOT text and drive. Trust me, it's not worth it! I know for a fact that you won't be able to live with yourself if you were responsible for hurting somebody, or worse, killing somebody because you couldn't wait to text. Accidents and deaths happen every day because people just don't get it! There's no way that you can pay attention to the road if you're distracted by something else. Even if it's just for a second, don't do it. Anything can happen in that split-second. I want you to drive with safety in mind. Keep yourself and others safe by doing your part to keep your eyes on the road.

Please DO NOT speed and race your cars like you're in the Daytona 500. I can't tell you how many teens I've seen doing this on the highways and in town. You're not only putting your life in serious danger, but other people's lives as well. You could lose control of the steering wheel or anything could go wrong. Vehicles aren't toys. Vehicles take lives all day, every day. It seems like whenever I turn on the news, somebody has lost their life due to a car accident. Most of the time, it's because somebody was driving too fast. I'll say it again, drive responsibly.

Please don't read while driving. I know some of you may be saying, "Reading?" Yes, reading. I see a lot of people actually trying to read a book while driving. Some people try to get last minute studying done too. That's not a very wise thing to do. Keep that in mind.

To the young ladies: Don't try to do your makeup while you're driving. Wake up early enough to do that before you get on the road. You and I both know that you cannot fully pay attention while trying to do your lashes, lipstick, eyeliner, etc. What good will your makeup be if you don't make it to your destination?

I know some teens love to beat-out their music, but it's very distracting. When your music is too loud, you can't hear what you're supposed to hear when you need to hear it. It's very hard to hear the ambulance when your music is on full-blast. I see ya'll sometimes. Your music is slammin', heads bouncing, and you're leaned far back in your seat. You've got to do better! Drive safe!

Absolutely under no circumstances do you drink and drive. It's pretty much common sense. Drinking and driving kills! It is simply not a good idea to do this. You may think that you can drink and drive while being safe, but that's called false confidence. Just don't do it! You'll be glad that you didn't.

I want to share a quick story with you. I had a really good friend and her husband had a drinking problem. He always thought that it was okay to drive after he'd been drinking. Well long story short, he got behind the wheel one night and he hit and killed a person while they were walking. He ruined his life just like that! He lost his family, and he's in prison for a very long time.

Do you see how fast things changed for him? He went from having a family, to losing his family and serving a lengthy prison sentence. It is not worth it! You could lose everything in the blink of an eye. Please take my word for it. I don't want you to ever have to experience this first-hand.

I know it's exciting to have your friends in the car with you, but please don't let them distract you either. Keep in mind that their lives are in your hands. Do your best to keep everybody safe.

Internet, Chat-Rooms, and Secrets

I'll be the first to tell you that I love the internet. For adults, it's very convenient for some of the things that we have to do. I like the fact that I can pay my bills online, order stuff online, make appointments online, and YES, I love Facebook and Twitter too.

The internet is a great tool, but I want to talk about the ugly side of the internet. Let's face it, all kinds of people surf and use the web every day. The purpose of me writing about this is to keep you safe.

Be careful who you choose to allow in your space. This does NOT exclude boys. Don't be fooled. Teen boys are a target too. You have a lot of predators online and it's their job to prey on teens. I'll try not to get too lengthy about this subject, but I'm definitely going to make sure that you have something to keep in the back of your mind.

Make sure that you stay mindful of what kind of information you share with others online. This can come back to haunt you. Never EVER give out your address or phone number to a stranger. Some of you may be saying, "Duh," but you'd be surprised at how many teens do this without thinking. Again, my goal is to keep you safe.

I don't care how nice a person seems online. Don't EVER meet up with a person that you've never met before in person. You don't know who you're REALLY meeting up with. You could be getting ready to meet up with a very sick individual. Anybody can come across as cool online, but that could be just a front to gain your trust in them. Many teens have chatted with strangers online and then met up with them just to find out that they're nothing like they expected, or the teen was never seen again.

That brings me to this point: It's not wise to be secretive about this kind of thing. If you do go off and meet somebody that nobody knows about, you're putting yourself in a very bad position. Remember, if nobody knows about this, how could you be saved and/or helped if something went wrong? Think about it!

I would not want to see or hear of you being lured into sex-trafficking, or held some place where you were forced to do things that no teen should experience. Believe me when I say this: Some people have some sick minds. Don't be so quick to trust somebody that you don't know personally. Chatting over the internet or in chat-rooms doesn't mean that you know them completely.

Here's another thing I want you to think about. Just because a person has shared a photo with you doesn't mean anything. How do you know it's really them? You don't! Some people are also really good with words. They know exactly what to say to get you to believe in them. They're very good persuaders.

If you have low self-esteem, please don't go online trying to meet people to feel special. So many things could go wrong. Trust me!

Holding on to those kinds of secrets could cost you your life. Think about it! What sense does it make to meet up with a stranger? It makes no sense at all. You could be walking into a trap. You could be getting ready to lose your life. You could be meeting up with an unknown serial-killer. You could be meeting up with somebody who likes to torture teens. The point is that you really never know who the heck it is that you're meeting up with. Please be mindful of these things that I've talked about.

I know you may have seen movies about stuff like this, but guess what, it could happen to you too! This kind of stuff really happens to every-day, normal people. I'm not trying to scare you. I just want you to be aware of what could happen. Make sure that you don't fall for something that could ruin your life.

That was then, but Look at Me Now

Okay, I gave this a lot of thought and I felt that it was the right thing to do. I'm about to open up and tell you about my teenage years. Maybe this will give you more appreciation for my writing. I put a lot of thought into my writing. It's important that my words mean something to my readers. Everything that I write about has to have purpose and meaning behind it.

Let's take a walk down memory lane. My hell all started in the 4th grade. For some odd reason, my face starting breaking out really bad. I had horrible acne, especially around my chin area and on the sides of my face. I mean, it was the worst of the worst. Some of you may know exactly what I'm talking about. Not to gross you out, but I had blackheads and whiteheads. On top of that, my skin was sensitive and easily irritated.

I remember how people would talk about me behind my back and to my face. I had several girls ask me if I shaved because I had bumps around my chin area. I was called ugly a lot and, to add to it, I was a really skinny at the time. My hair was very short and my teeth weren't that straight. There were times that I would go into my room and just stare unhappily at myself in the mirror. I hated myself! I hated what my skin looked like. People teasing me didn't make things any easier. Acne made me feel dirty and ugly.

I was smart, so people would ask me if they could copy off of my paper. Of course I let them do it because I wanted them to like me. I remember bringing candy to school to share with them too. I just wanted them to like me. I would even offer up my lunch at times. I would be hungry, but I would act like I wasn't when they asked. Yep, I went through all of this in the 4th grade. What a shame! Grade school wasn't much fun for me.

Things got a little better in the 7th grade because my acne cleared up by then. I was so thankful to my dermatologist. For once in my life, I finally felt good about myself. I could hold my head up high and walk with confidence. I started dressing nicer, doing nice things with my hair, and really putting effort into how I looked. I felt great!

Oh boy! Now, here comes the jealousy and bullying. Girls pushed me into lockers, threatened to beat me up all of the time, and would come up to me and say that they heard I was talking about them. Girls would say crazy things like "So-and-so said you wanted my boyfriend" or "I hope you don't think you're cute because you're not!" Here goes the hell all over again.

They didn't like me when I was ugly, and now they really didn't like me because I was cute and the boys all wanted me. I couldn't win for losing.

I got in a couple of fights. I hated that, but they left me no choice at the time. They just wouldn't stop, but once I fought them off, they left me alone. I didn't have any problems after that. I just couldn't take it anymore. I wish I would've spoken up at the time and told somebody what was going on. This could have possibly prevented that fight. Fighting was not my thing. I was never the kind of person who liked to start trouble or fight. That just wasn't my style.

Like I said, after I fought and took up for myself, everything was cool after that. I'm not proud of what I did, but it happened. I don't condone fighting, nor do I think that's the best option. That's why I talk so much about telling somebody. Get help and let somebody know what's going on. You don't have to go through it alone.

How could I forget to share this with you? I was raised by a single parent. I had a teen mother. To this very day, I've never met my father and I don't know what he looks like. I was the oldest of 3 siblings. My mother did the best she could with what she had at the time. It was a struggle in my younger years, but things got better in my latter teen years, as far as having money goes.

BUT, I do remember what it's like not to have or to not have enough of something. I know what it's like when your friends are going somewhere special but you can't afford to go. I know what it's like to want more to eat but there's not enough for seconds. I know what it's like to want more school clothes but your mom has made it clear that the clothes she's already bought have to last for the entire year. I know what it's like when all your friends are buying their lunch from the local fast-food places, but you don't have enough so you play it off like you're not in the mood to eat. I know what it's like to ask your mom for money but she just doesn't have it to give. I know, trust me I do!

I also remember what it's like to have to look after my sister and brother because I was the oldest. Because my mother was a single mother, I had to watch them a lot. I used to hate when my friends would knock on the door and I'd have to tell them that I was babysitting. I remember the time my best friend had a birthday party and sleep-over but it was cut short for me because my mom needed me to come home and watch my brother and sister.

Try to imagine that happening to you for one second. You're in the middle of having fun, and BAM! The fun is over that quick for you! I had a lot of chores around the house. Too much if you ask me.

We lived in East Palo Alto, CA which, at that time, was the murder capital. Yep, I lived in the hood. We later moved to East Menlo Park, but that wasn't any better. East Palo Alto and East Menlo were neck-and-neck when it came to drugs and killings. Imagine being in class one day with your classmate and, then the next day, you see their body in the streets lying there dead. Imagine liquor stores on every corner of your neighborhood. Imagine seeing people hanging out on the corners selling drugs and shooting dice. Imagine seeing your friend's mom or dad walking up and down the streets because they're so high on drugs.

This is the kind of crap that I grew up around. I was used to seeing police all of the time. It was the norm for me. Not to mention, every now and then, we would have somebody hop our fence because they were running from the police. Some people didn't have any respect for their neighbors. It could be really late at night and they'd still be blasting their music.

I know the struggle, but I'm so thankful that I didn't let that determine who I was going to be in life. So with that being said, if you are struggling right now, let your circumstances and surroundings motivate you to do better. You've got to push forward and make something of yourself, no matter what.

Through it all, my struggles have made me who I am today, and I am proud of myself! There's no way that I should be where I am today in life. I thank God for keeping me! I have a good life and I'm grateful for everything!

I'm going to leave you with this: Things may be difficult, but stand strong and don't let it break you down. It will get better in time. If you do what I advised you to do, maybe you won't have to go through as much as I did. I was afraid to speak up at the time but, as I look back, I know that things would've been different had I said something. Learn from my mistakes. Again, you don't have to go through it alone!

Through all of my hurt and pain, I rose to the top. I still can't believe that I've self-published 2 books. I have so many great qualities and so many talents.

That's how I want you to feel about yourself. Know your self-worth. Speak highly of yourself! Think highly of yourself! Be the very best that you can be! Make your life worth talking about! Make your life count! Live, and live well! You've got this! You can do it!

Unforgiveness and Forgiveness

I'll be the first to tell you. I know first-hand what it's like to live with unforgiveness in my heart. I'm going to share with you what I battled with and then explain to you why you have to forgive in order to move forward and live in peace.

I had a lot of resentments toward my mom, and my dad whom I never met. I resented her for having me at an early age and I blamed her for everything that happened in my childhood. I felt like I couldn't always be a kid because I had to watch after my brother and sister. I had more responsibility than a child should have. I didn't like the fact that I had to do what I felt she should've been doing.

On top of that, my mother wasn't the kind of person that hugged, kissed, or told me that she loved me. It just wasn't in her nature to do those kinds of things. So, I grew up feeling unloved by her. I never heard kind words from her. My mother never abused me physically or mentally, but she didn't know how to show love.

I resented my dad. Although I never met him and didn't even know what he looked like, I still wanted him to come find me. I wanted him to be in my life and be my dad. But that never happened. I always thought to myself "How could you know that you have a child and not come after him/her?" I'll never be able to understand that.

Over the years, I've battled and struggled with unforgiveness in my heart towards both of them, but I had to forgive both of them in order to move on with my life. It was the best thing to do. I had to do it for myself!

One day I decided that enough was enough. I was tired of being bitter and angry. I took the time to look at all of the facts about my teenage life. My mother was young, she didn't know any better. She did the best that she could. I couldn't blame her anymore. I had to accept the fact that she was young, inexperienced, and uneducated. What did she know about being a mother? She was a young-adult herself.

I started looking at the good in my mother and all that she had done for me and my siblings. Although she didn't hug, kiss, or tell me that she loved me when I was a teenager, she would make sure that we had a clean home. She didn't allow people to run in and out of our home. She didn't drink or smoke. She wouldn't even let her friends smoke in the house. They would have to go outside to smoke their cigarettes. She always made sure that we had food to eat, even if it wasn't much. She kept us safe. She made sure that we were always clean and nice-looking.

My mother and I have a very good relationship today. I'm so proud of her and she's proud of me. From where she started out, she shouldn't be where she is today. My mother does VERY well for herself and she doesn't want for anything. Every time I see my mother we hug, kiss, and tell each other that we love each other. That is our "norm" now. It feels good! We talk with each other and we enjoy one another's company. We take trips together and everything. My mother has a big heart. It's such a blessing to have her as my mother.

I thank God that she's an AWESOME grandmother to my only-child. My mother and daughter have a serious bond and love for one another. That makes my heart happy and full of joy! She's giving my daughter the love that she didn't give me when I was young. I appreciate and respect her for that.

As far as my dad goes, I've had to forgive him and move on. I found out from his side of the family that he battles with drugs, alcohol, and he's had his bouts with prison too. So, it was easy for me to forgive him. He obviously has some serious issues in his life. I actually feel bad for him. That's not a good way to live your life. But, I don't know his past. I don't know what has happened in his life to make him live the way that he is. I wish him well.

I feel so good now! It is such a relief to not carry around all of that unforgiveness in my heart. If you're living with unforgiveness in your heart, I would strongly recommend that you let it go. It's not worth it! It's not worth your happiness and peace within. You have to find it in your heart to forgive and move on. You have to do it for yourself! You deserve complete happiness within. You can't live in peace if you're holding on to things that are weighing you down.

Forgiveness is necessary if you want complete peace within. Once you forgive, you can work on building healthy relationships. When you embrace forgiveness, you will begin to rid yourself of anger, bitterness, depression, and all sorts of other unhealthy things in your life. Do it today! Forgive and let it go. It's not for them, it's for you. ~PEACE~

Best Wishes and a Note to My Readers

If you're reading this, I want to thank you for reading my book from the beginning to the end. I hope that this book has impacted you in some kind of way. I wish you the very best! I pray that you will move forward and do what you need to do to live the BEST life you can!

Always remember that you hold the key to your future. It's up to you to persevere. I believe in you and I know that you're going to make it. Not only will you make it, but you will be somebody that people will respect and look up to. Believe and aspire to do great things with your life. Don't settle for less than what you deserve. Move forward with a plan and work it out!

If you enjoyed my book and it has impacted you, please tell others about it! Help me get the word out about, *Teens Matter Most*. You can help me out by tweeting, mentioning me on Facebook, or just simply talking about it to others. I welcome you to connect with me on Twitter, Facebook, or any of your other favorite networks.

You can also tell your teachers about this book. It would make a great-read for school. If you know people who work with teens, tell them about this book. If you attend church and you have a youth group you're a part of, you can tell them too. There's so many ways that we can spread the word. *Teens Matter Most* is a book that every teen can benefit from. Let's make it happen!

When you're done reading *Teens Matter Most*, please take the time to go on Amazon.com and write a review. I want to know how my book has changed and/or impacted your life. I want honest reviews. I would love to hear your stories. As an author, I value and respect my fans and readers. Let your voice be heard.

Together with your help, we can make *Teens Matter Most* a best-seller.

Printed in Great Britain
by Amazon.co.uk, Ltd.,
Marston Gate.